THE VERSES OF A DAMSEL

SHEENA MARIAM THOMAS

Made with ♥ on the Notion Press Platform
www.notionpress.com

It takes almost a lifetime to know our potential,

but some people let you burn in the fire of glory and achievements.

Dedicated to,

The people who let my soul fly

to achieve its greatest heights.

Contents

Contents

Contents

Contents

Sometimes we cry to heal,

Sometimes we bleed to smile.

So, cry & bleed through a pen.

1. Be theirs...

Don't you have any pain??
A little girl's question made everyone stare with a smile.
An extraordinary bonding,
That's so weird.
But it happened.
"How can you shine so bright every day?
you haven't cried even once?? "
The sweetest voice that provoked them
With a brightening phase.
They replied,
The pains will make you shine more,
The tears belong to you,
Never show them to the world.
As that never going to be their concern.
Shine for yourself,
This is going to be simpler than it hurts,
It's going to be fine.
Regrets shouldn't be breaking barriers for you.
The wounds are to be healed as it is meant for.
The darkness should never prevail over you,
The light should be a way to the most beautiful path.
Your brightness should hold you even when the world stands against you.
Be the light to someone's path,
Be the hope of someone's love,

Be the relief to someone's pain,
Be the healer of someone's wounds,
Be the smile over someone's tears,
Be the faith in someone's dreams,
Be the power to someone's weakness,
Be the one among millions,
Be the unique one even in the crowd,
Be the star in the darkest sky who shines in someone's life,
And always give them a reason to live.
The star twinkled and fell on the earth.

2. The End

Some pains never leave us,
Neither do we leave them.
We find our paths,
In an undefined way.
Struggling for hope,
With a fake faith.
Truth makes the bitter part
And the lie into the most beautiful ones
But in the end, everything ends.

3. A Little Girl's Wish

It all started with a broken piece,

That gave hope to a little girl.

With eyes closed and head bowed.

No one to hold her,

She just made a wish!

Yeah!

The wish she made a few years ago,

Became the reality of today!

The dream which she saw a few years ago,

Became the happiness of today,

She is living,

Again and again

By holding her dreams,

And just a wish,

Which has been fulfilled by a broken piece.

4. Absence Of That Finger

That finger was enough for me

to hold,

To stand,

To dream,

To walk,

To stay,

The time was still for me then,

But today that finger was not enough,

For me to stand,

Somewhere in the light,

The absence of being alive prevailed,

And struggling to die......

5. Ms. Lonely

The world behind me stops
For no reason,
And the whole world had a pause
For a second,
The reasons were always undefined,
The reasons were always kept sacred,
The reasons were marked to be special,
Undefined, Sacred, Special,
All that are meant for the loneliest girl,
In the world of escapes,
The girl found a reason to live,
The girl found hope to dream,
The girl found herself amid a pause.

6. Remembering Her!

The time was still for me,
Till then and now.
That night,
With my eyes closed,
Remembering the time,
That will never come back.
Beside me was her body,
With the smell,
That is not of any flowers,
But the one that always awakens my brain.
Her body when in contact with mine,
The softness that heats my nerves.
Oh! wished I could have lived that,
Very moment again and again,
In my endless darkest life.
Her eyes that look into me,
always provoked me to hold her forever
Her lips are not red as a rose nor pink as a baby,
but it always made me long for the sweetest and tasty kisses.
She was not fair nor she was beautiful
But the cuteness of a baby never died in her.
Her hairs were not so long enough,
to play with it
but it always played with my inner deep feelings.

Her body was not perfectly curved nor she was sexy,
but whenever she came closer to me,
It killed me and those wounds became more beautiful.
Life with perfection was not her plan,
but her imperfections always made her specially imperfectly perfect.
I wish I could have lived it again in my life.
Not to explore her but to live for her and live with her.

7. The Solidarity Tree

To the sky who can see my tears,

Can you be mine??

To the burning hot sun who can my roughness,

Can you be mine??

To the dunes of the sand who can see my dirt,

Can you be mine??

To the wind who can see my sufferings,

Can you be mine???

To the illusion of water who can see my thirst,

Can you be mine??

Oh! I feel so lonely,

With a heart full of sorrows.

The solidarity laws,

Was my fame,

but that was too an end.

Can you be mine was changed forever to be yours?

To the man,

Whom I saw crying,

Whom I saw begging,

Whom I saw holding his pains,

Whom I saw breaking himself,

Whom I saw to be solidarity for no reason,

Whom I saw all alone,

Whom I saw wishing for something less and special,

Whom I saw asking for a soul who could understand,
I promised at last,
Which marked forever,
To be yours.
Can I be yours??
Was the hope I gave him till he died.

8. The Writer's Pen

From heartbreaking sadness to temporary happiness,
From the magical loneliness to the unfair crowd,
From the unexpected hatred to the impossible love,
From the silent soothing rhythm to the meaningful lyrics,
From the never-ending silence to the powerful noise,
From the struggles of heart to the blissful memories of mind,
From the void darkness to the colorful rainbow,
From the bleeding pains to the marvelous comebacks,
From the list of failures to the uncountable victories,
From the beautiful nature to the unpredictable mankind,
From the lullaby of a mother to the screams of a girl,
From the love to the betrayal,
From the hope of having someone to the fear of losing someone,
From the most special to the most simple,
From the faraway sky to the never-ending ocean,
From the untold stories to the magical mysteries,
From an imperfect life to a perfect love,
Yeah! All the mysterious imperfections were written by me beautifully.
Yeah! All the failures were marked by me as an experience.
Yeah! All the emotions were shown by me to the uncaring world.
Yeah! All the unsaid words were spoken through me to this imperfectly
perfect world of blank pages.
Yeah! I saw the beginning and the end of each writer.
Yeah! Till today they live and I make them alive each day.

9. A Pen and A Blank Page

The day ended, and a new page is beginning.
Somewhere I was scared.
The possibilities of being alone were more than being with someone.
Loneliness marked the most beautiful phase in my life,
And I never accepted the truth.
The world was still then and now,
There were no differences that made me low.
In the loneliest sky, there was something that always
Filled it's emptiness.
Maybe it's the sun or the moon.
Maybe it's the stars or the clouds.
Always a medium filled with the most beautiful
emptiness of this world.
But peeking into the emptiness of my life,
There always has been a pen that was filled with the ink of blood,
that always wrote what I failed to say,
That always filled the bank page with the color of pain,
Helping me to escape from the demons,
Holding me from the depth of my fears,
And that's true that I am not a writer,
Nor am I a poet,
But this is the only medium I always had,
My pen and a blank page,
With a heart full of untold mysterious stories.

10. Darkness...

Still remembering that night,
with no lights.
The whole world pushing me in vain.
Yeah! still remembering those beasts,
Who was waiting to suck my blood,
And the world watching in despair.
Still remembering the innocence that prevailed.
Within an immature heart and body,
to understand what happened,
The pain took a lifeline to start another life of vulnerability.
The scars were perfectly taken as a body part.
Yeah! I have been a victim of someone's thirst.
My body then and now begging to die.
The whole world called me as a whore.
With a smile, I went on.
The reason for who I am today is the world.
The so-called whore was created by this world.
With tears inside my heart and a smile on my face,
I went on.

11. That one step...

That night under 1000 stars,
struggling for life or death,
With the moon above.
Many more secrets to explore.
The fight was all set on fire.
With the burning ashes,
with a hope to start again.
I took a step back.
With tears of unmelted pain.
Deeper than the darkness.
With the eyes closed,
Again I took a step back.
But how long will it continue?
The questions never stopped my bleeding.
With all the strength I took one step.
But this time with a smile.
A smile to end up everything.
The step that never made me come back again.
The last step.
That one more step.
Which will decide my destiny in hell or heaven.
I wonder today,
What and who stopped me from that one step?
Why they would have?

With a smile, I started again.
But this time, the steps I took a little backward.

12. The Promise

To the world, I promise to be the strongest girl.
To the moon, I promise to shine brighter even with my scars.
To the sun, I promise to burn my fears and
with the fire, I will lighten up my world.
To the clouds, I promise to be smooth and
soothes the inner me.
To the trees, I promise to stand on my own and
shade my life and happiness.
To the sky, I promise to be the best even when I am alone.
To the butterflies, I promise to make myself
colorful and lively.
To the flowers, I promise to blossom my soul with joy.
To the raindrops, I promise to be the hope to
myself and faith that never dies.
Me, I promise to live for myself with
the dreams that took birth with every budding stage of my life.

13. Still, Awaken

To the world, that sleeps.
To my mind, that always stays awaken,
I am the one,
Who dreamt,
Who lived,
Who died,
Who suffered,
Who cried,
Just for a moment that is so lively and miraculous.

14. Nostalgia......

The shortest path of our journey.
The longest days of our memories.
The brightest hours of our togetherness.
The soothing minutes of our fights.
The charming seconds of our victory.
The formal meetings of our discussions.
The lasting epic of our success.
The caring bites of our food.
The sharing that holds our pain.
The nostalgic crumps of our room.
The supporting hands of our staff.
The melancholy strains of our fear.
The struggling beats of our events.
The vibrant smiles on our face.
Somewhere you and me, they and them, us, we, together made a journey.
With a perfect incomplete chapter.
The hope of being together.
Somewhere amid life.
Leaving the best part to be completed later......

15. You and me......

You are my sun which brightens up my life,

I am your moon which sparkles the best time of your life.
You are my rainbow which always
fills my life with full of colors,

I am your sky where you always stay.
You are my star which twinkles my world,

I am your dark cloud which sheds your pains as tears.
You are my shadow who always
supports me even in the little shade,

I am your darkness where you can
hold me closer without any fear.
You are my dew drops which always gives
pleasant feelings to my beauty,

I am your raindrops which hide your tears without exposing them to the
outer world.
You are my flower that always blossoms a smile on my face,

I am your butterfly which always makes you realize your sweetest taste.

16. Inner voice...

I cried till my tears dried.
I complained till I got relieved.
I wounded myself till I got rid of my pain.
I cursed till I got satisfaction.
I lied till my words became meaningless.
I fell till the smell of my blood carried me.
But still, I am in pain,
my heart is in vain.
My tears died within my soul.
My smile disappeared forever.
The colors of my life faded in the dark.
Now,
I am all alone,
Searching for a way,
Not to disappear but to find me.
To find the real me.
To find the reasons to live......

17. For you...

I want to be the breeze
that touches you gently & softly.
I want to be the sun rays
that make you shine more in my glare.
I want to be the raindrops
that hide your tears.
I want to be the mist
that makes your nerves chill.
I want to be the flower
that brings a smile to your face.
I want to be the light
that removes all your darkness.
I want to be the shadow,
that gives support to you in a little shade.
I want to be the sky,
that makes you admire the beauty.
I want to be the rainbow
that makes your life more colorful.
I want to be the star
that holds onto your dreams.
I want to be the moon
that shows your mesmerizing face.
I want to be the ocean
that takes away all your sorrows as the waves.

And at last,
I want to be your Butterfly
that always flies along with you to enjoy the love.

18. Saudade...

Those days and nights
with a memory that is stuck in my heart.
Finding ways to escape
& holding me tight to recover.
Somewhere I lived that moment
not once but as many times as I could.
Today I am dying for that one moment
As much as I can.
Hey you!!
Yeah! You gave me that moment
but it was long back.
Today that long back sucks,
Those longing kills.
Hey you!!
Yeah! you made me alive each second
but it was long back.
Today that long back hurts,
that liveliness destroys me
Hey you!!
Yeah! you held me and my pains,
but it was long back.
Today that long back makes me bleed,
that bleeding that never stops.
Hey you!!

Yeah! you made me smile,
but it was long back.
Today that long back brings tears,
The tears of pain.
Hey you!!
Yeah! you colored my dark world,
but it was long back.
Today that long back hits me like hell,
that breaks my heart.
Hey you!!
Yeah, you!!
You are the one I need!
You are the one I am longing for.!
Hold me so tight
so that you won't be a memory anymore.

19. As the river......

Like a flowing river,
My life went on with its flow.
Like a dancing river,
I enjoyed my part being on earth.
As the river beautifies its curved,
I owned my tears with a smile.
As the river flows with a dream,
I started my journey with hope.
Like a toddler river starting its journey without any destination,
I ended up with a new long-lasting start.
Like a stubborn river crossing each hurdle with ease,
I managed to keep up my track.
Like a soothing river refreshing all the beings,
I hid my fears for someone to revive.
As the river encloses the beauty of sunlight within itself,
I wrapped the darkness
holding the light of the moon within me.
As the river accepts the dirt of every being on earth,
I stood upright even with the body
that has been used for so long.
As the river,
I flowed with the dirt carrying deep inside the scars and
a smile to hide it forever.

20. It Was You

Even the darkest days
shined brighter than thousands of stars.
The most horrible dreams
were converted into a fairy tale.
The tears were turned to smile.
The fears were burnt in the fire.
Yesterday's life
Were transformed into the past.
The hopes of the future made me alive.
The world stood against me,
But you never allowed me to bow,
you held my hands with a promise of being togetherness.
The broken puzzle with its shattered pieces,
Again found a place to be fixed.
You loved me for who am I.
You cared for me for what I have been through.
You encouraged me for my good and bad.
You stood beside me with a promise.

You,
The well-wisher,
The best friend,
The soul mate,
The companion,

The partner

&

being in every role you moulded me
For who I am.

21. To the superheroes of every daughter...

With the falling feet,
you taught us to stand.
That one finger always gave us hope
to run towards you.
With the tears,
you taught us to handle situations with perfection.
With the fears,
you taught us to be strong.
With the bleeding wounds,
you taught us to smile.
With pride,
you taught us to salute our nation.
Falling, Failing,
Defeating, Dying.
All these always marked your strength.
With the power,
You taught us not to differentiate any.
With the hunger,
you taught us to learn the value of every minute thing.
With the thirst,
you taught us to value each human.
With the battles,

you taught us nothing is permanent.
With the victories,
you taught us the essence of love.
With your life,
you taught us to be the best...

22. I Bleed...!

I do bleed, bleed for a cause,
& bleed every month.
It hurts, but it's fine.
I do bleed, bleed for a reason
& bleed day and night.
It irritates, but it's fine.
I do bleed, bleed for a longing happiness.
& bleed with a pain.
It frustrates, but it's fine.
I do bleed, bleed for a life.
& bleed with a smile.
It fails, but it's fine.
It stops, but it's fine.
I do bleed, bleed for myself.
& bleed with a hope.

23. Oppositions today?

A dream seen by me,
was sown by my parents.
Changing lessons taught me to be strong.
A dream;
With 100 oppositions,
& non-valuable rejections.
It was just a dream,
when I alone held it,
stood alone with a hope that never tires.
Faith in me, I struggled by holding myself.
They do doubt me and my dream,
when they heard one yes and thousands of no.
Today it's not just a dream,
It carries a life and a hope for the better tomorrow.
Today they are holding me for a dream that I saw yesterday,
And for the rejection they made yesterday.

24. Cure By the Nature

To the world,
That listens and ignores.
The panic caused all around is going to end,
When you learn a lesson,
To be respectful to your land.
Nature is free now,
from the web of humans.
It's healing, the time may not be sufficient,
But it's getting better.
Each human falls today,
as the way you kill trees every minute.
The people are been caged,
as the way you caged those innocent animals.
The pleasures are no more but the peace surrounding now
is quite pleasant.
The mother Earth is saving herself,
From the crooked cruel humans.
Till yesterday, the suffering nature was our audience,
Watching us patiently and hoping for a change.
Today the opportunity has been passed,
To mankind now seeing the healing nature impatiently.

25. April Fool's Day

Dear me and you,
welcome to one another April fool.
The day for fools.
The day for fooling many innocents.
The most awaited day by many of us.
Just to be happy,
by making someone's feelings as a weapon.
This day is not for them…it's for us.
Yeah! It's for you and me.
In the land of betrayals, fun, enjoyment, and a license to play with
anyone's feelings.
Why do we need a special separate day?
Not only them.
We all are a fool.
This day is to realize and understand,
Didn't our life fool us somewhere in the midst which went unnoticed??

26. Wolf and the moon

In the darkest sky,

again, I saw your painful smile.

With the uniting souls,

again, we fought with the separating distance.

Your smile hurts me,

though you pretend to be happy,

I felt the pain of your deep scars.

The brightness of yours can make anyone blind.

But how you can hide from me??

The destiny united us with a powerful weapon of distance,

the land and the sky.

The wolf and the moon.

Each night I will be here waiting for you.

Each night we look into each other's eyes

when the whole world sleeps.

Each night our souls break the barriers by a hug and a kiss.

Our love will never die.

Because yet another night is waiting for us.

27. Childhood......

The world with a cute perspective.
The world was full of magical love.
The fakeness always seemed to be the truth.
No complaints, No betrayals, No discouragement,
No backing off, No hatred.
The world of perfect ugliness,
but still overloaded with fun.
The heaven on earth,
the never-ending happiness.
Imperfections made our efforts into a beautiful art.
The world of unknown fake reality.
The world of uniqueness.
The innocence that always gave birth to a perfect smile.
The mother's lap; a place for peaceful sleep.
The day always longed for a tiny walk holding
the giant fingers of our superhero.
Fairy tales were the real world there.
Lived a life of no regrets.
The world; full of chaos,
but always with a pure heart we made many smiles.
No failures, No success.
This piece of art gave us a reason to look back,
At an imperfectly made beautiful creation on this perfectly made day.

28. The unfair creation

Set by a goal.
Not to live, but to earn.
Learn to lead, not to follow.
Race of life, with an unknown destination.
Papers became more valuable,
Money became our priority,
and humanity seems to be disappeared.
The fire burning within us, set us to run
for the materialistic things.
Somewhere in between,
We fall;
The helping hands were ignored then and now.
The relationships went in vain.
When responsibilities took place.
Forgot to look back,
Where we lost the pretty tiny happiness
while chasing the hidden success.
Life is too short and it's a deadly truth.
Still, we are living, but with an unknown destination,
That assassinated our beautiful world.

29. The Sleepless Nights

The sleepless nights,

Holding myself to recover,

From the mistakes that haunt me,

Became yet another reason to stay awake.

The monsters who touch my soul.

The devilish noises that preach into my ears.

The eyes; full of tears,

The mind; full of fears,

Somewhere I lost myself.

Sometimes I lost control to catch my breath.

And now,

here I am, With a bruised heart,

Singing a lullaby to myself,

With a hope that this night too,

will end soon.

30. Greed & Deed

The shortest agreement,
lined with valuable love and care,
signed by an unknown person,
given to us to follow,
with countless responsibilities.
That was never implied by us,
That life always carried a reward;
a never-ending happiness,
surpassing those treasures to reach the top.
Running behind the world of temporary leisure,
forgetting that this won't come again,
and dearth of time for both of us.
A life begins with a cry,
It overwhelmed the whole world with its innocence.
but today the same tears overpower
symbolizing the overtaken greed and unpleasant deeds.

31. Made A Mistake!!

With a mind full of regrets,

with a heart full of pain,

I stood holding my life; full of mistakes.

The mistakes that haunted me day & night.

The mistakes that crushed my lively happiness.

The same mistakes that gave me a new start,

a new journey to my world of happiness.

A new chapter that was learned by myself

& taught me hundreds.

A new hope that directed me to a different destiny.

From that place, I learned destruction molds us into a most powerful one.

Lessons taught me that beautiful sculptures are sculpted by hurting them

several times.

The mistakes;

allowed me to frame myself.

So, by committing mistakes continuously

I was in the trail of achieving

&

by making mistakes I am alive.

Never give up!

32. Acceptance...

The deadly hell sprinkled the rain of peace upon me,
When my spines were breaking apart from each other.
The darkness becomes the light for a whole new life.
The tears of my pain sparkled in the heat of the fire.
The preaching noises were tuned into soothing strains.
The red eyes that always stared,
now filled with the tears of regret.
The hands which gave me pain yesterday
now hold me in my loneliness.
The deadly sins were forgiven once more.
The regrets again became the reason to live a better life.

33. The Change They Forced Me to.!

Deep inside the deadly soul,
I carved myself into a beautiful sculpture,
turned into a stronger soul out of pain,
that can withstand any kind of vain.
Deep there I placed a melting smile
that masked most of my tears.
The site of attraction,
The mesmerizing art,
The brilliancy,
The hard work,
The uniqueness
Depicted the most fabulous work
the sculpture caught the attention of passengers & warned those who
nettled me with pain.
Hiding the scars with an out-shown beauty,
Again, succeeded in tricking the people.

34. Dad's little princess....

With warm hands, you welcomed me to the world of unfair wars.
With a crown of being Dad's little princess.
Every hour spent with me seemed like seconds for you.
Every single tear of mine made you panic.
You being so rude to the world,
became a toy for my happiness.
Sometimes an elephant, sometimes a joker,
You perfectly personated yourself within seconds,
To make me laugh.
I forgot that day, but till today I can picturise in your eyes,
My first footsteps,
holding your hands as a courage,
I walked majestically with a smile.
Your hands never left me nor it allow me to fall.
I still feel the depth of your love,
when I called you "appa" for the first time.
The world that started changing around you,
was when your little princess started
her journey of growth towards life.
I still remember the hope you had in me.
Pedalling without support, you made it possible for me
With a word that gave me confidence
"Don't look back. You won't fall
because I am there to hold you"

Still, now I start every footstep toward my dream,
with hope that you are at my back.
The fear that I see in your eyes today,
Maybe ends up me falling into the deepest sorrows.
So, I won't look back,
For this time alone,
to your eyes that always hold me to you,
Because your little princess,
wants to be a Queen of this world tomorrow,
with her father's hand still holding her,
but this time with a proud smile and warmth
That this queen still resides in me
With my little princess within.

35. SHE

She may not be the beauty of your views,
but she's pretty in her way.
She may not hold you with her words,
but she always has something good to say.
She may not be the hub of everyone,
but she loves what they are.
She may not like fights,
but she's a warrior in her life.
She may not seem to be a little princess,
but her dad is always a king to her.
She may not be a melophile,
but she always has that melancholic air to sing.
She's a unique piece of art.
Which only a pure heart can read.

36. She is my MOM

More than being busy, I let myself free.
When the world was busy,
Struggling to learn the art of earning,
I was enjoying the art of living & that's too from a housewife
who seems to be less educated, perhaps less creative.
From the smile of others to her sweat,
I felt the most breath-taking art in her foods.
Who distinguished a housewife and a working women based on their
creativity??
After all they both are mothers,
who knows to serve even in their hunger.
Today the artist seemed to be less creative,
in front of a mother who was pouring love,
with utmost passion on her food,
which going be served soon.
Yeah! It's true that,
Making a dosa is also an art,
The smile and the love added the tastiest flavors that no one could ever.
The perfectly round chappatis were also
an amazing piece of art,
Which was made without any compass.
From the pinch of masalas to the pinch of love,
The quantities were perfectly measured
without having any measuring plates.

The way she chopped vegetables
was also really an exciting view,
Because even with the utmost speed
all the pieces were the same size.
She always has been a wonder for me,
Even though she is not an artist nor a super-women,
But still, she always had the magic at her fingertips,
That served us with the art of a beautiful mother.

37. With you, it started......

It all started with you,
Even though the binding of two bodies,
leading to the formation of a big spherical ball,
scientifically I am just an embryo,
but for you, I know, I am your life.
After all, it started with a dream you saw,
the pain you underwent for several months,
the monthly weakness that leads you strong to bear me.
It was closed and dark when I began to breathe,
More than me you felt the tiniest growth of my body
step by step.
Unknowingly I came into you,
But knowingly you were holding me forever
even when the barriers were strong.
More than my heartbeat, I felt yours.
More than my pains, I felt your tears.
More than my happiness, I felt your smile.
The world was you, for me.
Then and now.
Somewhere in the midst, I fought,
We misunderstood each other,
Argued out of my ego,
Just to win a fight with my mother.
Still, you held me in my pains,

Suffered along with my worries.
After all, it started with you,
This journey of my life,
With a hope that you sowed a long year ago.

38. The Forgotten Love

The days of happiness went somewhere so far,
Maybe beyond the sea or the sky,
Got into the search for that pearl, in the depths of the ocean,
With a hope, to start a new day, same as those days.
With popping hundreds of love you messages,
With the lapse of time concise,
thank you and sorry messages.
With the never-ending conversation
not even knowing the topic.
Now became silent even with lots of topics,
from Miss You to Do You Love Me,
Converted the scenario of a beautiful love story,
Into an obnoxious one.
From the real to the fake smile,
Somewhere we both adjusted to each other.
Somewhere we both managed to accept rather than expect.

39. You Made a Change by Leaving!!

Is this the world you wanted to live in??
Is this the world you dreamt of??
Is this the destiny for which you worked??
Is this the day for which you live today??
Today you live for someone,
who never care for you tomorrow.
Today you accept someone,
who will leave you somewhere in the midst?
Today you believe them more than you,
who will degrade you even at your best?
Today you will shut yourself and make them shout,
who will slap you tomorrow even in your goodness.
Today they will decide and you live a life,
full of opinions and suggestions, led by someone
who never even hugged you in your sorrows,
who never even pat you for your success,
who never even accepted you as who you are.
In the end, you will apologize to yourself,
for not living your own life.
You will cry,
but the same person will smile at you,
a sarcastic one,

for which he had won,
And making you fail.

40. Maa, maa...... Maa....

Happy Mother's Day maa.!!
Can you hear me??
Or should I shout some more??
Today you are looking awesome.
Do you know how long I have been waiting for you to wish??
Today I missed you.
From the morning,
All showed their love with status and a story.
But I wanted the tears to flow,
the pain to show.
The remembrance of that destiny,
leading a barrier of heaven,
Making you shine as a star in the sky
& here I am standing on the land
Not even remembering your face,
As a helpless hopeful orphan.

41. The reflection...

I saw you today also,
but you seemed to be lost.
Your eyes had the fear,
your lips trembled to speak,
your tears mixed with the water,
that made me fade.
Your hands had a different taste now,
that made you dwindle.
Again, I saw you &
now you were more visible than earlier.
The fear was burning to strength.
The trembling voice gave life to a soul.
The dried tears glittered your beauty.
Your smile made me beautiful.
Even from the other end,
I felt your breath.
You found the person whom you were searching in me,
And I found the person who made me alive in you.

42. A Girl to a Woman.

Locked in a dark room,
Screaming for life,
Hoping for someone to save,
Holding myself to stand,
Crying to make me strong,
Faking a smile to replenish my soul,
Telling myself the lamest excuses to escape from the fear,
Dreaming for the tiniest sparkle,
Reviving the happiest moments to get back to my life,
Starting each day with a strength,
Surprising myself with the minuscule claps,
Beholding the little girl in me,
I was becoming the woman for an undreamt tomorrow.

43. Bravery

Holding a family picture in one hand,
And a rifle in another, set for a goal,
Which destined them to death.
The war fields weren't new to them,
nor gave them a reason to fear.
Holding the pride of a son & the love of a father,
They ran to the land of fire and blood.
Even holding their decisive breath,
with a proud smile & honor
they sacrificed themselves,
to the mother India.
The spirit was buried with salutes &
in a most prestigious manner.
The world lost a brave soldier.
a son lost a hero
who called him Little Champ,
a daughter lost the king
for whom she was a little princess,
a wife lost her loving companion
who crafted fondness with her,
a sister lost his naughty brother
who supported her in all crises,
a brother lost his buddy
who was the reason for him to be cool,

a mother lost her son whose smile was
the happiness of her life,
a father who lost his pride and who never allowed him to bow,
and the history made yet another bravery
into an immortal pride for tomorrow's nation.

44. I did it.

Walking to an undefined destiny,
holding the pictures of yesterday,
fixing the paths of mistakes into righteous,
differentiating the cruelty from goodness,
serving the poor with the torn money,
faking a smile even in catastrophe,
directing the hatred to love,
leading me to the toughest times,
parting the precious treasures to the wanted.
Returning with the success that stays,
hearing him saying " I am proud of you ".
The legacy that made me strong.

45. Why hm...?

Hm…Hm…Hm…
It sucks and it's a feel.
It breaks and it's a hold.
It humiliates and it's a care.
It confuses and it's the root of conversation.
It haunts and it's a smile.
It shatters and it's a hope.
It breaks and it's love.
It provokes and it's an emotion.
It damages and it's a part.
It ends and it's a void.
A miraculous void that speaks,
holding the anger and softness,
carrying the sadness and happiness,
breaking the healed,
& making the worn-out,
with just two cute little letters,
The 'H' of hope and the 'M' of miracle.

46. Our India...

From the land of powerful colors to the land of blood.
From the land of hopes to the land of betrayals.
From the land of unity to the land of wars.
From the land of beautiful greeneries
to the land of deforestation.
From the land of education to the land of corruption.
From the land of natural resources to the land of pollution.
From the land of quality to the land of quantity.
From the land of love to the land of hatred.
From the land of democracy to the land of racism.
From the land of protectors to the land of rapists.
From the land of development to the land of destruction.
From the land of peace to the land of priorities.
From the land of humanity to the land of money.
Somewhere, we too changed.
The from and to became common.
The scarcity became customary.
And the betrayal became traditional.

47. The warmth......

The warmth that always gives us comfort.
The warmth that always promises togetherness.
The warmth that holds our strength.
The warmth that never leaves us alone
even when the whole world stands.
The warmth that always stops us from falling.
Is the best part we can hold forever in our hands.
Feel the warmth.

48. A Distant Love

From a distance apart,
our souls carved a way to be together,
In a most unexpected way of love.
To love and to care
seeking the presence of those unseen smiles
through a drop of tears.
Somewhere my soul yawned for you
hoping for a better day
to eradicate the absence.
Somewhere your soul made a perfect healing,
for the bleeding wounds of mine.
Sentencing to death became more fair
than the distancing presence
with hope we again waited
For this dreadful day to end.

49. Will Win!

Don't feel low, you will win,
but today was not your time.
Next is your turn, you will win.
With a smile, she replied:
Today I failed,
but I failed for a reason.
My failure is a success,
My failure is my growth,
My failure is a lesson for me to be humble,
My failure is a judgment of my talents,
My failure is a way to know me,
My failure is a fact to accept anything,
My failure is a great teacher for a better tomorrow,
My failure is a victory made within myself for trying,
My failure is the smile of the person who won,
My failure is a hope for someone else to try again,
My failure is me,
myself stepping towards the greatest victory.
Not letting you down, I will win.
Today I won again,
On the race of life again, when I learned to
accept the bitter circumstances and the truth.
The father sighed,
With relief that her daughter

learned the most difficult chapter of her life.

• 63 •

50. Hey, is there anyone named God??

Hey, is there anyone named God??
Mesmerized with the question,
I went and asked her
Why do you want to know about him??
The little voice shot a desire
that be fulfilled by the so-called God.
Unknown to the answer, I replied to her,
Yeah, you can find him in the scoldings of your mother,
In the smile of your father,
In the eyes of a cutie pie like you,
And where you have hope,
You can see him, sometimes within yourself.
You can feel him,
Wherever the promises are held to bind us stronger.
Your wishes will be fulfilled,
When you believe him.
And she ran to hold those tiny fingers,
She found the God in the baby
who was lying in her mother's lap?

51. To Smile!!

The mirage of constancy,
To the careless movement,
They too taught me the matter of life,
Nothing stays constant,
Nor the problems nor the pains.
The void of silence,
To the dreadful noises,
Again, they gave hope to my silent life.
The devilish darkness,
To the purity of white,
It again showed me the switch to the lights of hope.
The crying colorless clouds,
To a beautiful septa rainbow,
They again took me to the colors of my smile.

52. Fight With the Past

Holding the past,
I want to run somewhere so far,
But I chose to stay, Stay for a reason,
That was never defined nor understood.
Leaving the past, I would have lived for the present,
But I chose to hold on to the past,
Hold on for a reason,
Those were the guilty scars on my soul.
Drying the tears, I would have laughed at least for once,
But I chose the tears to flow,
Flow for a reason,
That was only meant to me.
Hoping for the best,
I would have owned the victory,
But I chose the failure,
Failure for a reason,
That was the worst nightmare I have ever had.
I would have chosen the smile rather than the pain.
I would have chosen the acceptance
rather than the expectations.
I would have chosen the me in myself rather than the others.

53. The Birth of a Mother

The smell of stained blood,
The pain of an unsaid happiness,
The new journey of a little life,
The transformation of a girl from a wife to a mother,
The smile that always bloomed in her,
She too was enjoying being in care,
Those tiny movements,
Unfelt breaths,
Spontaneous growths,
Were felt like magic within herself.
The time seemed to be slow,
The wait longed her too vain,
But today, the day has come,
When a part gets separated from her,
With the birth of a mother too.

54. A Thought with A Pen in Hand

With a pen in hand,
Holding the thoughts of yesterday,
Staring at the paper with a smile,
Hoping to start with something good,
Again, bounced the questions,
Asking to myself,
"Where to start and how to end?"
Not knowing,
The answers were still similar rather than familiar,
"Don't know."
Was the striking mind undoubtedly throwing,
Dreamt of making history,
With a life that was familiar rather than similar,
Again, my emptiness held me to my thoughts,
And made me realize once again,
That this isn't made into a history,
rather it's a lesson to be taught to hundreds by thousands.

55. Choice For Truth

Hotness or chillness,
A mother or an infertile woman,
Death or an unknown future,
Real or fake,
Mine or theirs,
Tears or a smile,
Decent girl or a sex worker,
Failure or pride,
Dependent or independent,
Fight or the calmness,
Yeah, I chose the second,
To know the transparency,
That leads to miseries.

56. Mother India

The stars on her shoulder,
Pride on her head,
She walked majestically,
Towards the unsolved wars.
A dream in her eyes,
The hope of her father,
She became the queen of a little Princess.
A soft-hearted mother to a warrior woman,
She held herself to be best in both.
The sparkling smile of her kid,
And the bravery power of her mother,
Gave birth to a caring mother and a strong daughter,
Who fought with herself for her child,
And with the world for her mother India.

57. Who Am I?

With the secrets,
That causes the transparency about her,
Towards the unfair world,
Walking through the lane distant road,
Along with the blood-sucking demons,
Chants that have been continuously running,
With a great deep breath,
She held her clothes with a shy,
Asking herself,
"Am I a girl or a boy ??",
With the struggles that killed her for so long,
The never-ending battle of doubts that defines her character,
Those mocking smiles that linkers where ever she goes,
The abusive words that describe who she is,
Being a girl to satisfy someone &
not to be meant to become a mother,
Suppressed herself to the smallest circle of her agony,
Depressed for not being able to live,
Decisions that took to sell herself,
To the demons who just see her as
a slut that is meant to be used,
With a deep breath,
Holding her dreams,
With several unanswered questions,

She ran to save,
But not her,
A trans woman like her,
Who should not lead themselves
to end their beautiful transparent creation,
To a world that has been opaque to the truth and goodness.

58. The Only Happy Truth

Making someone feel special,
Were neither impossible nor difficult,
Letting yourself free,
Building you into a stronger pillar,
Baking someone's tears into a smile,
Spreading the positivity of yours,
Mesmerizing the beauty of your ability,
Destroying the negatives and cages,
Trusting yourself,
Needs that courage to own the smile,
Yeah, it's true that to make someone happy,
You need to be happy.

59. Destiny

Yet another year,
Came and passed just like that,
Holding you from the deepest scars to the endless smiles,
Making you stronger to stand & fearless to fight,
Yeah, this day also passed,
With the wishes of many loved and caring people,
With the prayers that smoothen your awaiting challenges,
Yeah, yet another year is waiting for you,
To make you succeed,
To heal you,
And to teach you to ease the hurdles.
Let this be your last wish,
Let this be your last prayer,
On this wonderful day of yours,
Letting all the fears vanish,
enlightening your smile,
Brightening your tomorrow,
Letting all your dreams flourish,
Making your destiny the way you dreamt.

60. Growth of Light

Years passed by,
From a baby to a boy,
You walked through all the softest paths,
Holding your father's and mother's finger.
Those tiny fingers were safe in their hands,
Like a pearl in the shell.
Again, months and days passed,
With an excitement in their hearts,
You've grown into a teen.
Holding your dreams in a smile,
You walked to overcome the hurdles,
Without holding those hands that safeguarded you once.
Your growth has been an impulse for them,
Holding their fears within themselves,
They saw you growing,
Growing up with a destiny that isn't meant to be destined,
They saw you roaming, crying, frustrated,
But never allowed their anxiety to touch you,
because they know that today you are a strong man,
Having these many years passed like a cloud,
And showered the rain of bad and good know-hows,
That made you stand strong,
Holding those weak wrinkled hands
into your grown-up fingers that once safeguarded you.

61. Stay for a while…

Stay, just stay.
Stay for a while,
Not to hold you forever,
but to bid the last goodbye.
Stay for a while,
not to make you mine,
but to teach me that you no more.
Stay for a while,
not to convince you,
but to convince me that you went so long.
Stay for a while,
not to make me smile,
but to have your smile with me forever.
Stay for a while,
Just stay for a while,
So that I can have at least your name,
With mine.

62. A Crusade in You

I saw the real me in you again,
Holding the past to the future with an unpleasant present,
Hiding the fear,
In a drop of tear.
The smile managed to cover the pain,
The days that usually went in vain.
Today your bare skin too felt shy,
Even though I am yours, then why?
I saw your body shivering,
And those lips trembling,
Hoping to escape from something,
It went hiding,
made everything into nothing.
Let yourself free,
So, you can fly,
So high,
Letting yourself to burn in fire,
Making you into a hard weapon.

63. Soul Mate

Let them talk to me,
Those beautiful eyes that eagerly waiting to see me.
Looking deep into those black holes,
I felt the secrets that are awaiting to explore.
Even your breath asks for my smell,
I denied to hold on to you,
Just to make you breathe harder to own me more.
From you, I found my soul mate,
That existed just for me.
The dead unspoken soul that was buried so long,
Awaked with your love,
That never dies anymore.

64. I Let You

I let you leave me,
For the reasons that can't be explained,
And for the pains that can't be the bearable ones.
I let you leave me physically
From a world where success marks the connection
And money makes the relationship.
You were still in my thoughts
Wanting to stay there itself
Letting to go somewhere so far
I let you live in me
Secretly buried in the graveyard of my thoughts
Away from the materialistic world
Our souls rejoiced to be together
I let you leave me
For the rebirth of my immature young soul.

65. A Blessed Dream

Far away from the world,

The scenario hits my head,

The earth with its greeneries,

Letting the creatures be so lively.

No deaths no pollution

No more struggles

No more fights

The world with its simplicity

Not letting the plasticity

To rule over us

Is this just a dream??

The smiling earth with no more plastics.

66. Human, The Demon!!

Clean crystal clear,
Not letting the world be pure.
With dirt that lies inside and outside,
In humans and the earth.
Pollution-free or a package of pollution,
We decide the worst.
Making even educated thoughts a ruin
Reuse or recycle,
We ignore both just to lose.
Degradable cloth bags,
Become extinct in the era of plasticity.
Artificial greeneries,
That became more effective than natural
Caged creatures finding a way to be bound to the earth
Making homo sapiens
the extinct harmful creatures in the museum.

67. Chose to be Fools

The existing present,
That always haunts the future.
We made it mandatory,
To focus on results,
Rather than our satisfaction.
We plead to win the race,
Rather than accepting the pace.
Letting ourselves down,
We failed even in success,
Making the pride to stay,
We exist the true self of ours,
Somewhere, in the depths,
We fought for the results,
Rather than our potential.

68. Bleeding Memories

Dropping the shells of solicitous,
I jumped onto the shore of productivity.
Letting my life go on with its flow,
I made all my nightmares to blow,
Hoping for a new start,
But the destiny carried me to a torment.
That thrashed me to bleed.
With a contrasting verdict
Which wasn't ever predicted
The renascence of a girl
With a perplexing phase
Distant from the liaison
Concealed within a sacred essence
A solitary mother was born
Once again to bleed.

69. A Girl in The Wave

It went on like the waves of water,
Hitting my legs and the shore,
The tap of distinct objects,
Petrifying the breaths,
The time that doesn't heal,
The rhythm of beats,
When he came close,
The eyes never lied,
But she chose to hide,
That it doesn't hurt her anymore.

70. K a l o n ...

The beauty in my eyes
Which never fakes.
The unread tales of my scars,
That is always covered with the bars.
Those sacred prayers
Which went unanswered.
The darkness that holds my identity
meant to be my tranquillity.
Fighting to search the beauty,
I made my smiles hideous.
The nights and the days
Never escaped from my ways,
To find a destiny
Which was always mine.

71. A list of broken things....

To the most beautiful soul on this earth,
who broke down to see that smile on my face.
her dreams were still alive
but kept hidden somewhere deep within herself.
With the shattered pieces of hers, she smiled.
She smiled to hide the most beautiful pieces of her pain,
she smiled to gather herself in a most haunted way.
The pain was not new for her,
but the smile has been always.
She was broken and being separated
from her soul like the way how the sea and seashore;
the sky and the land;
the moon and the sun;
the love and the hatred;
the life and the death.
She was finding the missing pieces of the puzzle within me.
The more I smile the more she gets happiness.
She finds each piece of hers when I win.
The failure of mine even beautified her puzzles.
The more I fell, the more she gathered courage.
Yeah! She was finding the broken pieces of hers in me.
She was the most beautiful soul on earth who taught me to smile with a
broken and unsolved puzzle;
who gave a hold not to stand but to stay;

who made my haunted place into heaven;
who gave strength to bear pain with the hope of finding the broken pieces
in someone like hers.
Yeah! She is the most beautiful soul on the earth.
My mother.
My angel of broken and unsolved puzzles,
Who broke herself to put me together & complete.

72. The Change in (me) Love……

Today I'm totally a different person
with all the colours of love over my body,
With all the delightful memories in my heart;
With no fears of regrets,
With a smile on my face every time.
The spark of life;
The songless wonders;
You made me what I am today!
I carried the secrets of nature along with you,
flew for the sweetest nectar of nature
I smiled till the end
I kissed the sun with my wings
At last, I closed my eyes by capturing
All the beautiful spectaculars!!!

73. Unsaid Words

Miles never separated us
Nor do the situations.
I fall for you,
As do you fall for me.
Pains caused the barriers
to build the wall of separation.
Words struck within me;
which I always wanted to say.
Your love killed me.
To the world I paused,
Why do I?
Paused for a second or a minute,
But it took the lifelong agony.
Today you are not meant for me
Nor do I!
But a picture always captured within myself,
The world that was written in my heart,
And I promise you
One day you will feel my presence
Presence even in the absence.
Love even in the hatred
Smile even with the tears
The world will change that day
For you and me

An unsaid love story
That all started with a pain
And ended with a smile of emptiness.

74. That Person

To love and to be loved,
Is something precious.
To care and to be cared,
is something special.
be the light to someone's darkness
was taught by someone special
Yeah! he taught me,
to be the moon in the solitude sky,
to be the brightest star among 1000s,
to be the breeze of hope
he is the one,
who held me before I fell down
left alone along with the world
just to teach me to stand on my feet
Yeah! he is the one,
who give birth to my dead soul
who brightened up me with his words of love,
who promised to be with me
who gave the power to fail
who consoled me before I wept
who encouraged me before my action
Yeah! he is the only one
who gave me everything
just to see me fine.

Today I can fail,
stand-alone,
conquer the world,
win the battle of fear,
enjoy the pain,
because everything lies within me.
Yeah! he is the one,
who burnt the tear of failure
who made me believe;
that I can burn the evils
Yeah! he is the only one
the special one has
the only brother whose spirit never dies in me.

75. A Change Within a Day

Yesterday

I started with a lie,

Happiness was melted in the tears of pain,

Love vanished with the appearance of hatred.

All the trust was broken into pieces like a glass

I was alone with all the regrets and pain in my heart!!!

Today

I started with a truth,

Tears of pain now turned into tears of happiness,

Love again proved to be stronger than any hatred

The broken glass of trust was replaced by

new one with hope.

Loneliness became my happiness with no regrets.

76. Dark Side of light

That day;

There was no rain,

no darkness,

no chillness,

There was not even a single drop that induced those feelings.

But still, it happened

Only because of the reasons that can`t be justified,

She was a girl and they were men,

Only because she was alone and they were more in number.

She wasn't mature to be used,

But still, she got the pain at the age of 8.

But still, she underwent the worst thing.

But still, she felt harmful touches.

But still, she was crushed inside and outside.

Today she is no more,

But her soul will be wandering around us,

Just to save a life like hers.

But our unfair world instead of helping her,

Struggling for the beasts like

who crushed her into the ground,

The sparkling lights of this world.

77. My First Love

You're my first love,
You accepted all the pains just for me,
You would have felt very happy on that day,
When you came to know that you're going to be a mother!
From that day you must be smiling every second,
Even in your pains with a hope that you can see me!
You felt all my touches when I was within you,
You felt all my emotions when I was within you,
You felt all my growth when I was within you,
I too felt all of yours and his soft touches,
I too felt your pain but never bothered.
I see your smile each time when you think of me.
I felt all your emotions when I was there within you.
When the day came when you were waiting,
you smiled even in your pain.
The tears of happiness said a lot of untold emotions.
You made your blood into milk to feed me,
I started growing by seeing your smile,
You always held me whenever I fell down.
Days went your little girl started to feel her pains,
She became matured.
You were happy but not me.
You taught me to smile even
if I'm in lots of pain I learned to smile!

But, whenever I smiled artificially,
you can only understand,
the way you ask, always made me cry &
share everything with you.
I thought everything changed, but still, now nothing changed!
Miss you Amma!!

78. The Gift of My Life…

Today I realized,
Best friends are forever,
Because of you!!
A friend like you,
Is hard to find.
Tough to have and painful to lose.
You're like a sunshine.
Who showed me the light of love,
When I was in darkness.
You're like a flower.
Who always gives me the nectar of happiness…
You're like a butterfly.
Who always showed me the beauty of life…
You're like a soul.
Whose spirit will never die in me..!
You were always there by my side,
Who wipes all my tears,
Bruised away all my pains...
Today each smile on my face,
Shows the sign of your friendship
Each joy of my life signifies your importance in my life...
I never like you,
Because I always loved you a lot!!
Today I can lose anything but not you;

Because you are someone I could never replace!!
Everything changes in our life,
People go and come in,
But,
I want you to stay always with me by my side,
Because you are truly an extraordinary gift!!!

79. A Day for The Father

You were one among the millions,
And yeah! that was for me,
A father was born along with you
On that rainy day.
That awaited moment,
Still lingers like a spark.
Your first cry,
Still echoes in my dreams.
Your soft skin,
Still pushes me back to that time,
When I gave birth to a person,
Who was hidden somewhere so deep?
Your smile,
Still makes me to sense of the past,
Feel the present
&
Prepared for the future, with you always.

80. The Phoenix

The desire to grow,
Within the fire of burning ashes,
Were drained into the hopeless lineages,
That determined the aptitude of a girl
Struggling for peace.
To be something
That needs to be latched
Within the four walls
Like those barricades.
Compelling the mastery
Into a household stature
In afraid of burning others
Wiping out those dark smudges
Still committing to a designated tag
Marking the end of every pursuit.

81. Togetherness

Holding your hands
Feeling your sweaty palm
Stepping into destiny together
That you notched
Once long back
Where you stood so empty & stubborn
But hope to its fullest
An asset or a liability
That wasn't ever defined or detailed
Making the nothing
To the power of something being together
Somewhere you dreamt bigger than us but only us
Which was meant for us only.
Only for us, created by us.

82. Those words...

Those slow-moving nights
Those teary eyes,
A peep from another room,
Was always a hope,
That wasn't ever fulfilled.
The scary haunting nightmares,
Those howling voices,
A pat from another person,
Was always a peace,
That hasn't ever happened.
The sleepless dusk,
That deadly darkness,
A word of togetherness from my person,
Was always a dream,
That never came true.

83. An Exotic Bloom

The blood-stained dreams
Like in her white saree
She outraged like a princess
And the lioness in a birdcage
She neither stopped nor gave a setback
Against the world
She stood lone
With a piercing sight
That burnt even the ashes to fires
Within the cage, she led herself to glow
With the limitations marked
She broke the cage.
Set herself free.
She gesticulated herself to be the top.

84. The Precious Time

I tried to hold,
I fought till I could,
Not making it to go so long,
It will stay
The thought made me so vague
Formulating the constructions
To the verge of destruction
I held it so long,
Wasted enough to regret.
You can't judge when
a future turns present & present to past.
Devoid of the reality
That it won't stay
Neither for you nor for me
Because it has to go on
Without a pause,
Because time doesn't cease for anyone
So, make it worthwhile if you still have it.

85. Smile for the Pain

Each darkness is marked by a sparkle of light.
Each dusk ends with a lovely hopeful dawn.
The rain has stopped for a beautiful sunshine
with a signature of the nature.
The thunders have ceased to be once for a benign start.
So, as the pain,
Once in a while, the pain has to be washed away
for a mesmerising smile.

86. Shattered

It went on,
Like the pearls of a broken chain,
Shattered here and there,
Some are hidden,
Struggling, sweating & bleeding,
Pearls & blood together
Making the spot so vibrant
Leaving the translucence floor
Into an awesome-colored one
Fostering an art by itself
Sometimes giving a hope
To every heart
That once shattered.

87. My True Self

In the world of glowing beauty,
Just to get attention over.
I chose to be the dusky damsel
With neither the shine nor the flimsy,
That carved only the simplicity
Making a unique creativity
That never fades nor dims,
Just only to expose my true self.
Even in a world where a unique one is named as an odd.
I fight to be my true self not devoured by society.
I chose to be the opaque objective
Over the world of fake transparency,
Whatever it takes.

88. NEVER PROCRASTINATE NEVER COMPROMISE

Everything you dreamt is destined to be your success.
You may collapse without any hope.
But never ever forget the reasons
for why you struggled and travelled this far.
NEVER PROCRASTINATE
NEVER COMPROMISE

89. The Lost Soul

Deeper the pain,
Stuck in vain.
I bowed day and night,
just to make myself right.
To the flawless ways,
that darkens my rays.
With the soothing voice,
I made a choice.
To stand for myself,
that strongly went against ourself.
Holding the scars,
within myself.
I found a smiling soul
That was just living with originality & the reality.

90. The So-Called Justice?

Distance can't be measured,
but we talk about measuring love.
The future can't be ever predicted,
but we talk about unpredicted care.
Past can't be forgotten,
but we often insist on forgetting the scars.
Destruction can't be stopped,
but in this era, we talk about destroying humanity.
Relations can't be safeguarded,
but still, we try to safeguard our egos just to make someone to fall.
Failures can't be ever accepted,
but the world forces girls to accept the rapists.
Pains can't be bearded,
but the people want you to accept the life long-suffering
just because you are a girl.
Life can't quit itself,
but we always quit our potentials
just because of some stranger's word.

91. Herself

Let her fly,
To the world she dreamt of.
Let her fall,
To learn herself to raise again.
Let her fail,
To guide herself win tomorrow's race.
Let her run,
To train herself move relentlessly.
Let her cry,
To mould herself indestructible against the wicked.
Let her burn,
To prepare herself winged like a phoenix.
Let her fight,
To attain her destiny.
Let her bleed,
To make herself a woman.

92. A Mother from Mother

Fights without an end,
For the reasons without any logics.
We two were separated,
From the boundaries of our age
& the interests that were so opposing,
but somehow our souls are connected,
with an umbilical cord that wasn't seen anymore.
Fake hatred always,
The crossing over of arguments,
The extending weeps over silly complains,
The limitless explosion of words,
Somewhere in the midst,
We cared for each other,
Unknowingly and sometimes secretly,
we cherished for being sisters,
within the time lag of forever.

93. Everything Flew

It wasn't a happy ending,
& ours wasn't a perfect love story.
The dramatic world,
Neither found a uniqueness
Nor a tight endless bound,
but for us
It has been special always
& wasn't meant to be partial.
Those beautiful fights ending into
an understandable night,
Cuddling into each other's arms.
The warmth that I felt
Still making me melt,
Even in the memories of yours
The long back which was ours.

94. BLACK

The mate of darkening days,
The sensation of sleepless nights,
The aura of failure,
The determining facet of dark complexion,
The breath of fear,
The personality of boldness,
The demise of hope,
The moaning sobs of losing,
The companion of loneliness,
The urge to lustre,
The origin of dawn,
The advent of a mastery,
Black isn't just a colour,
It's the tome of an art.

95. With Love -Memories!

Far from home,
A distant untravelled road was made an option,
For every one of us,
Taking our life into an agreement of tomorrows.
From dependent to an unrelated independency,
That carved our liabilities to an asset.
Withholding the smell of our guardian,
Reserving the taste of those sacred dishes,
We set ourselves to organize,
Into the most established manner,
Making those perpetual moments to stay with us,
We took a stand that was distant from our memories.

96. Again, So Powerful

Being crushed & scrambled,

Lying there without an owner,

Marking the lineages of every line,

Making the intensity of its pain,

Enduring all its flaws,

With the falls,

Before an onset,

It made its demise,

Due to the enigma of its leverage,

But it was an outlet,

For a passing stranger,

Who made it a weapon of his writings.

&

a writer was born again.

97. A Book, A Day

The smell that hallucinates
the mind that starts the race,
To run furthermore,
To scrutinize the climax,
The silence which led to destiny,
That made every vein tighten up,
With the flowing time,
Bizarre to the surroundings,
Falling in love with the lines,
That clingy sound of turning pages,
That was set randomly,
Compelling the emotions one by one into a chunk,
Drafting the characters to the real kingdom,
Again, a book stole my day.

98. Life Falling Apart

Every then and now,
Failed to achieve,
Skipped every catch,
Holing the melancholic strains,
I again drowned in the depths of my miseries,
When will everything be fine?
A younger self asked with eyes full of wisdom,
Without breaking her hope,
I let her know the bitter truth,
That life is not what it looks to be and not a fairy tale which it could be
lived with,
Everything happens for a reason,
But yeah, this is what life is all about.

99. Just Another Phase of Love

Why does love always have a full stop in some of the phases?
Why can't we love someone who is ours or just have someone we love forever?
Love is a phase nut what is the phase after that to be called?
Why love is so painful?
Why do we need to love someone?
Why did we expect them to love us back?
Why don't we just accept the one-sided love and enjoy the phases alone?
Why do we need the other person to hold us, care for us, and pamper us?
Why do we always need them to prove the love they have for us?
Why these love are cliches?
Why it couldn't be as simple as those falling leaves during the autumn or maybe why it couldn't be so soothing as the blooming flowers during the spring?
Why is a separation always needed to prove our love?
Yeah! It is true that most of love is been successful then what about others?
My question is why not all the loves could be a successful one.
If destiny is already been decided then why we are falling on someone from where we couldn't ever get up?
If destiny is the end of all this then why could we even start something that is never been meant?
Why does this love have to be complicated?

Why it couldn't be as simple as undefined destiny?

100. From the Writer To the Reader

Dear you,
Just take a look for a perception,
That's how beautiful you are.
Your complexion never made you ugly,
But yeah, your overthinking will.
Your tiny eyes never wanted to weep,
But yeah, your worries will.
Those lips never felt of shutting,
But yeah, your own limitations will.
The hands that never stopped helping
Would have inquired more than once,
just to take a look.
Those beautiful fingers have always crossed
during every request,
Made an art of holding the prayers.
Those legs never stood for a break,
But you always denied hearing their tiresome pains.
The smiles,
Yeah, those smiles of yours,
Making beauty out of traumas,
Made me still for hours,
Gazing at the moment,

Not enable to capture forever,
It stayed like an inkling agony.
Your potentials never made you fail,
But yeah, you do fail yourself many times,
Not letting the voice to reach you,
That keeps on shouting:
"You can, you can just do it, you can."
Just take a look,
You will find an amazing piece of art,
That you perfectly carved long back,
With all those imperfections, madness
&
ridiculous nature of yours,
That left a little sparkle in other's life.
Just take a look.
A Request from your soul.